The New Message of Love, Book 3

The Healing Journey

Moriah

Copyright 2019 All rights reserved.
ISBN: 978-0-9709461-4-0
International Institute For Human Empowerment, Inc.

The New Message of Love—Book 3
The Healing Journey

A Gift from the Teachers of Love to Humanity

The New Message of Love is given in order to prepare Humanity for the New World in which Humanity is but one of many races in the greater universe. New communication skills, new methods of discernment, and the divine universal energy of Love, will be your guide and protection.

The Teachers of Love are high-vibration Beings, also called Angels. This following is their message to Humanity as received by Moriah (Sue Kidd Shipe).

The New Message of Love provides the context for what is occurring:

Book I. **Invitation to Love** invites us to join in concert with those in the flesh and beyond who are leading during this evolutionary change.

Book II. **Journey to Love** is a curriculum that will guide you to develop the necessary skills, perception, understanding, and power to survive and lead.

Book III. **The Healing Journey** provides a view of life as it goes through the stages of healing to true unity or oneness with the Creator, referred to here as Love.

Spiritual Empowerment will be your protection.

You are invited, wanted, needed, supported, challenged, and loved. Welcome.

Dedicated to the Provider of Unseen Assistance

Recognition:

Book cover: Erica Shipe Dodd, B.F.A.
Layout and design: Jody Morgenegg, CustomWebCare
Editing: Ruth Kellogg, Ph.D.
Photography: Sue Kidd Shipe, Ph.D.

The New Message of Love was recorded as received from the Teachers of Love over a period of 30 years. These highly evolved angelic beings speak through their Messenger named Moriah. It is now time to make the Message public.

The Healing Journey was received many years after **Invitation to Love** and **Journey to Love.** It defines Healing, takes you step by step on your Healing Journey, and shares Moriah's own journey. Moriah began, like you, as a student of **The New Message of Love.** As she took each Step, more was revealed to her. Each Step on her Journey brought her into deeper understanding through Experience, and prepared her to dedicate her life to bringing **The New Message of Love** to you.

The Healing Journey is life unfolding. It is designed for your highest benefit, bringing your life into alignment with Love. May it bring Love to your fear, Presence to your loneliness, Guidance for your choices, the Joy of fulfillment, and the Peace of Spiritual Empowerment.

The New Message of Love by Moriah, is comprised of three books. All are available on Amazon by author Sue Kidd Shipe, Ph.D.

Book 1. Invitation to Love
Book 2. Journey to Love
Book 3. The Healing Journey

You can learn more at:

www.thenewmessageoflove.com
www.enterthenewworld.com
www.newworldempowerment.com
www.newworldempowerment.org
www.humanempowerment.org

Follow our Facebook pages for information and events:

Moriah
New World Empowerment Center
New World Empowerment Ministries
Moriah's New World Library
International Institute For Human Empowerment

Join with others
Facebook Group:
The New Message of Love

Contents

I. Introduction to The Healing Journey

II. What is The New Message of Love?
   1. The Healing Journey
   3. Bringing It All Together
   8. Open to Healing

III. Your Healing Journey
   11. Reflections 1-40

IV. A New Paradigm of Spirituality
   54. Our Healing Journey
   57. Life is not an Empty Slate
   60. Healing of the Body Requires Healing of the Mind
   61. Universal Energy for Healing
   64. What is Healing?

V. Moriah's Healing Journey
   66. Healing Surrender
   68. Healing Message of Love
   69. Healing Evolution
   70. Healing My Soul
   71. Heal Me
   73. I Believe in Love
   75. At Peace
   76. Commitment
   77. Gratitude for Being

VI. Benediction

I. The Healing Journey

Introduction

"It is a most difficult task to persuade other humans of the need to prepare. This Preparation from God is revealed as Humanity goes more deeply into the universal evolution required to move from a global tribal community, to one of the communities of the greater universe. We will explain.....

Your people want to know why. Why is the climate changing radically? Why do I feel so ungrounded? Why do I want to escape other humans? Why are many seeking refuge and family with pets? Why do some hold onto outdated beliefs, both religious and scientific? Why do people try to recreate or destroy childhood memories? Why are some people risking life and career to warn and assist others? Why is the world becoming more dangerous? What can I hold onto? What will make me feel centered and whole? What will ground and strengthen me? Why do so many live with increasing anxiety? What are the "new" diseases? Why is pain increasing? Why are people choosing not to live, and not to bring children into the world? Why is there such disparity of resources? Why is trust crumbling in all areas? What can we do?

At times of great change, people struggle to maintain equilibrium. They find it very challenging to move forward, and they have less patience for self and others.

People need an anchor, even more so during great turbulence of change. It is even more challenging as trust fades in the institutions which have signaled stability: homes, families, government, schools, religion.

As those foundations are shaken, new anchors must be developed to assist during this great evolutionary disturbance.

Consider this: Imagine that you live for many years on a small island. You are the only human. Your life isn't easy, but it is predictable. The day is spent doing what is necessary to survive. You hunt and prepare food. You watch out for hungry predators. You seek and make shelter. Your days are consumed by activities needed to live.

One day, other human visitors arrive. They don't look like you. In fact, you don't really know how you look to others, but they are strange. They make unintelligible noises to you. They have different habits. And you do not know if they came as friends, or predators.

This is the condition now for Humanity. Humans have believed that they are alone in the universe. Now it has become clear to many that being alone was only an illusion, based upon one's experience. Humans, for all their individual differences, look much alike, yet humans have erected walls to isolate themselves from each other. They have built walls of social class, geographical boundaries, and beliefs. As these walls are brought down, humanity is preparing for a New World in which humans are but one group of intelligent life.

Like the one person on an island encountering reality-shattering proof that he is not alone, Humanity, too, is facing mounting evidence that Others have come and continue to come here. The Others are curious, and they are exploring. They have obtained samples of Human DNA for their own purposes. Their purposes are survival, and evolution. They have moved beyond their species identity, and come for many reasons. There will be no common language. Humans will need to rely upon instincts, long abandoned for more sophisticated communication.

Humans are not equally aware of the evolution that is occurring. Without awareness, they cling to superstition and dogma. As more humans "wake up" to the reality of this global, universal evolution, there will be much fear, disrupting violent behaviors, and philosophies of "live for now", or "escape the world". This is not necessary. A Preparation is given for the safe unification of our worlds, but Humanity must first learn this Preparation called, "The New Message of Love."

Humanity is on the threshold of an earth-shaking, paradigm-breaking, event. This event will re-write history as your people learn truth when they are able to clear their minds of dogmatic beliefs, and see what is really occurring. What has been, is, and will continue to occur is the exploration and unification of Humanity with the Other intelligences of the Universe. Indeed, much is occurring in sight that is still hidden because the human mind filters out that which does not fit its paradigm of reality. We will explain.

A child is born with an open, inquisitive mind. At birth, there are new experiences such as seeing, feeling touch, adjusting to temperature fluctuations, hearing sounds beyond the sounds experienced in utero, and tasting and consuming food. The child is making connections with these experiences: I like this. I don't like that. Hunger, loneliness, and eventually fear enter the child's consciousness. The baby takes in new information and its brain draws conclusions.

As the child develops, it is aware of the values of the parents and caregivers. Some behaviors are regarded as good; others are forbidden. The child's own value system is simultaneously developing, and forming judgments: right, wrong, good, bad, acceptable, unacceptable, delicious, unpleasant.

As the development continues, the child is exposed to lessons that reveal the parents' beliefs. Many children attend and belong to a specific religion whose values are acceptable to the parents. Thus, the child's concept of reality is being developed. This is a simple, yet effective, way to look at how a person develops over time into a youth, and then an adult. If during this time only current paradigms (generally accepted beliefs) are introduced or experienced, the person's view of reality, or the way it is, is perhaps unquestioning. It now forms the foundation upon which life choices are made.

Unexamined, unquestioned "reality" is the widely accepted view of what exists. When events, or experiences, or new information challenge the person's paradigm of reality, growth begins. However, this growth may take time and many more experiences before the person sheds his belief system in confusion.

Here is where struggles and challenges often create difficult situations which may lead to destructive behaviors, or may develop into new philosophies and beliefs.

It is at this point that the adult child separates from the parental beliefs to move onto a path of discovery. This is a challenging time for families, often wrought with misunderstandings, feelings of rejection, and accusations of lack of appreciation. Some people may change careers. Some marriages may not withstand the changes that the "developing" person may make. Communication often suffers, even when dialogue is continued and pressed. Families suffer as the changes may divide them. It can be a very painful and frightening, yet exciting, time. Each person continues to develop, if sometimes separately.

There are primarily two paradigms of reality that are causing great conflict within relationships at this time. There are people who have experienced, and continue to experience, paranormal events that do not fit the generally accepted view of reality. That reality is not yet open, but is opening to, metaphysical experiences such as seeing, hearing, feeling, and exhibiting abilities not developed by most humans. These people are generally not believed, and when they continue to speak on these metaphysical abilities and events, they may be condemned and shunned by society.

At this time, as the numbers have increased of those with psychic abilities and experiences of consciousness that cannot be explained by the current paradigm of reality, these people are uniting. People find safety and solace in the company of others having these experiences, yet are often shunned by family, friends, and work associates. Many hide their knowledge until they find an "appropriate" time to "come out of the closet." The price one pays varies, but many must walk away from those who no longer can accept them.

The great divide in your world at this time is not political and partisan. The divide is between those who still accept the general view of reality, and those who cannot accept this view but have a more inclusive view. Those with new open paradigms of reality are your new leaders. They do not necessarily have political power, but they have great political influence.

Your institutions are based upon the generally accepted view of reality. It is what they teach. It is what they stand for. They are being challenged, not by other humans or countries; they are being challenged by new beliefs and paradigms of reality. As this "new" paradigm develops which incorporates all the experiences: UFO's, Others (aliens), psychic abilities, channeling, direct divine guidance, visitations, teleportation, remote viewing, and ways of knowing through intuition, the institutions are challenged. When the tipping point is reached, the institutions will crumble. Already that is occurring. Traditional education, religions, medicine, science, psychology, parenting, governmental and political leadership are all impacted by lack of acceptance. Each is questioned, challenged, and often rejected. However, the dilemmas for those who no longer accept the current paradigm is, "Where do I belong?"

If one cannot teach what is required by the curriculum. If one can no longer limit medical treatment options to those within a current medical paradigm. If one no longer maintains a perception of the Creator that one was taught. If one no longer is accepted by friends and family—one is bereft of a sense of belonging, and thus protection. One must find new friends, belief systems, medical treatments, educational curriculums, and methods of parenting. And one may be forced to make these necessary changes while still responsible for growing families.

That's why New World Empowerment Ministries was born. That's why Moriah is bringing a Preparation called, "The New Message of Love." That's why this ministry is designed to minister to All Beings, to accept people of all abilities and beliefs, and to help people understand and practice the Preparation for this New World.

You, whose reality can include the unexplained, will be called upon to assist in this evolutionary change. The New World moves beyond the static paradigm of the past, and creates a new paradigm that continually expands with new information and awareness.

If you are reading this, it may be because you have heard, seen, or experienced that which cannot be true in the old paradigm of reality. If so, please continue to find refuge and solace in knowing that you are not alone, and you are needed to help humanity prepare for the integrations of many worlds and universes. We are not at the beginning, but we are far from the end. Join us as we prepare for the New World through the Preparation, "The New Message of Love", given to Humanity through Moriah. This Message provides us with the skills essential to safely navigate the new and coming challenges."

II. What is The New Message of Love?

The New Message of Love is a Preparation for Humans to join with others who are not human.

Humans long ago covered instinctual responses with politically acceptable behavior. By learning to deny our gut responses, we also lost some of our self-protection. That is why those who study human behavior in order to manipulate us, such as con men, are often successful.

Energy precedes intent. Intent precedes action. Too often by the time we identify another's intent, it is already too late to protect ourselves. Therefore, by learning to recognize the energy that surrounds and is in a person, we can better protect ourselves from negative intent.

Imagine you are in a group of people. Even within a small group, note which person feels inviting, who feels cold or disengaged, and who feels repelling. What is repelling you? If not words, actions, tone of voice, or body language, then what? Is it, perhaps, the energy that person carries? Note how you feel with each person, even if you do not engage them. When you leave the group, note your energetic experience with each person. Did it draw you closer? Feel like boundaries were protecting? Or repel you? Keep in mind that you, too, carry energy and others are responding to that energy.

Love energy, or spiritual energy, is very powerful. As the person on a spiritual path deepens his or her commitment, the energy becomes stronger. As a Step on the path is taken, the energy increases. As your energy increases, others may have stronger responses toward you. Some will be drawn closer, some will pull away, and some may even strike out. Keep in mind that when a person strikes out verbally or physically, with no apparent reason to justify such an action, it is likely the energy you carry that evokes this response. The perpetrator is not even aware of why he or she does not like you. They may create a story of how bad you are to justify their actions to themselves.

Consider Jesus the Christ. He was full of Love energy. He carried so much Love energy that people were drawn to him for healing and the Message. Yet those without loving hearts or carrying Love energy, questioned his motives and saw Him as a disruptive force. They killed Him because of the Love He carried that inspired His words and flowed energy to heal the sick. **They had to see Him as evil to justify their own feelings and actions.**

Those brave people throughout history, who carried great love and wisdom, were not accepted. They were seen as a threat because love is often seen as a disruptive message. They had followers, and appeared anarchistic to those who feared losing power. Many were destroyed because others could not tolerate them, their Love energy, and their words. Yet, their Message of Love lived on.

And now it is time for another Message. The New Message of Love is a gift from high spiritual Beings, called Guides or Angels. This is their gift to Humanity, given through their Messenger named Moriah.

THE HEALING JOURNEY

All life is about healing of the separation from Love, and the return of the soul to wholeness, or unity with the Godhead. Human life is about seeing oneself as separate, and taking a path to reach this state of union. Many are unable to do so. They fall away in lives of recklessness, shallowness, and living in the spotlight while simultaneously hiding in the shadows. They will join in another lifetime.

Life is about choices. One may choose to join and return Home, to the Source from which one came. One may also choose to remain separate. Thus, the Invitation to Love is the invitation to return to union with one's Source. Journey to Love is the soul's curriculum for joining. Life is The Healing Journey, and encompasses all of the roadblocks, twists, turns, rising and falling that are part of each life.

Life appears chaotic. In reality, it is a system of blocks and victories. Those steps that one overcomes are victories. Those that remain unaccomplished or unhealed are blockages. Therefore, the challenge of one's assignment on the earth-plane is to discover one's uniqueness and separation; decide whether to accept the Invitation to Love, and thereby begin the Journey to Love; and to encounter each challenge as it presents itself. One can use each challenge to propel one to victory, or to allow oneself to become stuck, and unable to go forward. In each life, the opportunity to surrender one's life to a greater power is given. The evidence of one's choice can be seen by their behavior.

You have seen those who encounter multiple challenges: sickness, loss, disability, and yet are able to say that it is their relationship with God, or Love, that moves them forward.

You have seen those lost to drugs, risky behaviors, and the dark side of Humanity. Alone, they feel abandoned. Desperate, yet unable or unwilling to surrender, they make choices that are detrimental to themselves and others. Their blatant disregard for the pain they cause drives them deeper into addiction and denial. Unless an intervention effectively convinces them to abandon their self-destructive path, they fall away into further illness and denial.

At this time, Humanity is facing a crisis of this decision, and its resulting losses. It is clear that an intervention that awakens Humanity is on the horizon.

Bringing It All Together

The Healing Journey begins by recognizing that we are all One, and the barriers that divide us are caused by our own creations. Humans created language. Within that language system, we created divisions, categories, and endless exceptions or explanations to further describe those categories. Take the word Love. There is Love meaning Universal Energy Source from which we all sprang, and to which we shall all return. There is the meaning of love as it refers to parents, spouses, partners, friends, offspring, pets, and continues, to lesser degrees, to those for whom we feel slight affection. There is romantic love, and there is acquired love. There is love between a parent and child which can be severed in the body, but never severed from beyond.

Love is an Energy. It moves from person to person, uniting them at any of a variety of levels. That is the distinction that was previously described, but also refers to a greater love for Humanity. There is love of country, which is the principle upon which that boundary-contained mass of land and people exist. There is love of ideas and philosophies, and there is love of religion.

Some people have said that religion has caused more wars than any other reason. That is problematic, as religion is constructed to teach people to, by whatever path, follow Love. The great spiritual Teachers and Leaders followed Love and urged their followers to do the same. Yet, it is the very principle upon which religion is founded that gets lost when people judge one another as "less than" due to affiliation.

Language is often the great divider, and although efforts have been, and are continually made, to articulate meaning even more precisely, words can divide. For this purpose, we shall look at the life of Jesus the Christ.

Jesus was unique because he was both human and divine. In his divinity he could see the frailty of man, and forgive weaknesses and poor decisions. He understood human ego needs for gratification, recognition, and power. He taught that Love was mightier than any ego needs, and challenged followers to follow Love. He did not ask to be put on a pedestal and worshipped. He asked his Disciples to follow him, and do as he did: heal the sick, raise the dead, love one's enemy. When the divide he caused became unbearable to some, he was destroyed in order to destroy his Message. However, the Message survived and thrived.

It is possible that the Message has become interpreted and enshrined in such a way as to make it difficult, perhaps impossible, for followers to grow. As we have witnessed so many exiting the construct of Christianity, it appears often that it is done because the individual chooses to grow and allow for more direct spiritual experience. What if people could grow and develop through these established great religions, but see them as occurring within the necessary time periods, while recognizing that spiritual infusion into our world has continued and today is even magnified? People are reporting evolution of consciousness in all areas of life. Electronic communications allow people of diverse faiths to communicate, and that communication is at times increasing the divides, but often helping us to acknowledge our common Humanity, and our need to reach toward unity with God, Love, Source, Universal Energy, Higher Power, or by whatever name you prefer. It is the emptiness in one's heart that causes one to reach for more, and it is Love that fills this vacuum in the soul.

If we choose another word, Consciousness, by which we express the desire for and subsequent reaching that appears to occur at some point in each life, we have a common word for a familiar experience. If we think of consciousness as something akin to water level, we can see in very simple terms how it works. All Humanity is within this sea of Consciousness. It expands and contracts constantly. As individuals, through Love-connection, or God-connection, raise their individual consciousness, it raises all. Conversely, as one follows one's lowest motives, all are affected. Thus, the level of Consciousness is fluid, and can become somewhat volatile.

Consider the effects of an act of violence. The anger it evokes causes the individual to first want retaliation. Retaliation may bring satisfaction to some, but it also increases the overall violence, which affects the level of Consciousness. As many turn to prayer for assistance and caring for one another, the level of Consciousness then begins to rise. The level of Human Consciousness is the total of all individual consciousness. Thus, in history, when Human Consciousness is low, an intermediary Spiritual Being appears to lead Humanity out of that darkness. This has happened repeatedly in history, and has led to many great religions. However, in spite of their teachings, once again the world is in darkness, with great challenges between light and darkness, good and evil. Which will prevail depends greatly on the direction of the level of our combined Consciousness.

Consider that humans, due to our own greed, callousness, and deceit, have created our world as it exists at this moment. If you are one who wants to move our world toward Love, you can assist by moving your own Consciousness toward Love. You can accept the Invitation to Love. You can do the spiritual practice called Journey to Love, and you can be part of The Healing Journey. As you make the decision to accept this Invitation to Love, and begin the daily curriculum of Journey to Love, you begin to raise your consciousness, which, in turn, begins to raise the entire Human Consciousness. That is why you hear spiritual leaders tell you that if you want to change the world, it is essential to first change yourself. The New Message of Love has come to show you how, to give you the way. *By taking this spiritual journey, you are at once affirming your religion by recognizing that it brought you to this point, and now you are able, with it as your firm foundation, to take the next step in your individual spiritual journey.*

A great religion is the initiator. You are now ready to begin the journey Home.

Much will go with you; much will fall away as you become this beautiful person bringing light to darkness, love to fear, and joy to emptiness. Your circumstances may not change, but you will change within your circumstances. And as you evolve, all that is needed will be provided. You are never alone.

Open to Healing

Healing is the acceptance of Universal Energy. It is the heart opening to allow this. It is the recognition that all of life is recorded in one's energy system. All recordings are attached to human emotions. All emotions are recorded in chakras. Therefore, when the chakra system becomes overloaded, illness occurs.

Humans exist within Universal Energy. It is around, over, and throughout them. Universal Energy is the environment in which all life exists. Therefore, when chakras become clogged or depleted, Universal energy can clear and fill the energy vortexes.

All food is energy. It is metabolized to become energy needed by the body. Thus, what is ingested is food for the body, and subsequently, the mind and soul. Therefore, the food energy taken in interacts with the body characteristics, and can itself promote health or dis-ease.

As you ascend the vibrational ladder, your physical needs change. Foods that are compatible with the vibrational level cause health and improved feeling physically, mentally, and emotionally. However, more dense foods must be released in order to allow the body optimal functioning. As you see others devoting their lives to their spiritual purpose, you may note that they have made dietary changes due to increased awareness of others' suffering, or increased suffering within their body-mind system.

As you move forward in Love energy, note all that supports your journey, and release all that no longer serves that purpose. As you progress, healing is essential so that the spirit is nourished and in turn desires service. Note those who are healing; you will see a new or renewed desire to serve.

Allow healing to occur. Release all that does not support your journey: food, activities, relationships, obligations, and beliefs. Healing will occur as you abandon self-defeating thoughts and actions. It is so ordained.

III. Your Healing Journey
REFLECTIONS

Reflective questions are provided here to assist you in **Your Healing Journey**. After a brief meditation, write your thoughts on the space provided following the question.

It is suggested that you keep a separate notebook available with you at all times to record healing thoughts as they come to you. And now, Your Healing Journey......

1. What have I learned in The New Message of Love that has added joy to my life?

2. What is my biggest challenge with The New Message of Love?

3. Who can assist me?

4. Who is having difficulty with my new choices?

5. Who can help?

6. How can I better use my time for spiritual practice?

7. What were once my dreams?

8. What happened to my dreams?

9. Where in my life do I feel most fulfilled?

10. What do I see that I want to improve?

11. What is my Spiritual Purpose?

12. Where can I find help with my Spiritual Purpose?

13. Do I see others working toward this Purpose?

14. What people or organizations can help me?

15. Does my primary relationship support my Spiritual Path?

16. Do my family members support my Path?

17. Do my friends support my Path?

18. Am I alone on my Path?

19. Who can help me?

20. Where can I find support?

21. Is my place of spiritual practice welcoming? Comfortable? Inspiring? Quiet?

22. What can I do to make my place of Spiritual Practice support me better?

23. When I am rejected, where can I turn?

24. Have I surrendered to Love?

25. Am I willing to surrender again?

26. Can I make an anniversary date of my surrender/commitment, and celebrate it annually? What is my date?

27. Is there something I can wear as a symbol of my Commitment to Love?

28. Am I willing to invite others to join me?

29. Who can join me?

30. Who is unable to join?

31. Can I find the strength to deal with rejection?

32. Can I find the strength to keep on going?

33. What resources do I need?

34. Do I believe that "what is needed will be provided"?

35. I commit to my Purpose and Calling in the world.

36. I surrender my life to Love.

37. I will go where I am called.

38. I will invite others:

39. Love will sustain and guide me.

40. I am never alone.

IV. A New Paradigm of Spirituality

Healing comes to us when we least expect it. While we wait, after seeking healing, events and people create new opportunities. When one has been hurt or rejected, the pain of rejection is healed when one accepts oneself as more important that the judgments of others.

The life you are living now sits on top of the experiences of previous lifetimes in a body. The shame or pain one feels in this lifetime is actually a re-wounding of wounds from previous lifetimes.

Pain is universal, as Love is universal. Fear and its progeny (doubt, uncertainty, and projection of negative emotions) follow pain of rejection. Physical un-ease in the body can sometimes be related to accidents or illness in previous lives. In other words, life in the body is a continuum. That is why when one achieves healing in one lifetime, similar wounding from previous lifetimes is also healed.

Love is an energy that sears through dis-ease, interrupting the status quo, and lancing the poisonous negativity within. It is as if Love lances the negative stored energy, opening it to burst out of its encapsulation, and drain. Once negative energy is drained, one is now ready to fill the empty space left behind with Love energy.

Unexplained actions or events can also create the opportunity for healing rigidity. As one holds firmly to the religious teachings from youth, one will have experiences that directly negate a part of that prior teaching. This challenge to one's faith is most confounding. At first, one is often able to explain away, deny, or deny the implications of the experiences. However, memories of the experience, or more experiences, can belabor the issue, causing much internal disruption for the person. This internal conflict continues, often becoming more insistent and uncomfortable, until one experiences a shift in one's perspective, a change in one's belief paradigm.

Sometimes at this point, the person leaves organized religion, or searches other established religions. This becomes a spiritual quest for truth. Internal conflict may continue until one realizes that "reality" is more than beliefs framed in an unyielding structure. Now one's true journey has begun. It may take one to new heights of understanding, or, may lead one away from spirituality and religion as disillusionment overtakes the person.

At this juncture, new explanations are often sought. It can be a period of great personal growth. It can also leave one bitter at the world and at those finding comfort in their new understandings. This is the choice one makes. One either accepts Love in all its forms, and moves forward on one's healing journey, or one remains stagnant until another lifetime and invitation are received. Thus, the healing journey is life, healing is available, yet free will requires the person to choose internally which he or she will follow.

Allow yourself to be open to new experiences. Allow an open and personal interpretation of these experiences. Experiences are designed to teach us what we need to learn. All new learning about Love moves one forward on one's path. And so it is.

Our Healing Journey

In the beginning we awoke in the womb. Already we were learning and preparing for a life of service. Our destiny was determined by our parents, and the environment into which we would enter the world was designed and waiting. Already a religion, or none, was part of our learning tree. Already much was determined regarding our status, access, health, and predetermined expectations from family.

We learned before birth to experience sound, pain, comfort, security, or lack of security. We absorbed into our consciousness the relationship of our parents to one another, and knew before birth if our existence was welcomed.

Already we knew experiences of parental and other anxiety. We carried memories from other lives and before birth. We were an awakening consciousness with memories of lives and lessons. We began where we left off: some lessons learned; some to be learned.

We brought our unique consciousness into a waiting world. It had experienced death and new life before. Some relationships were renewed; others left for yet another lifetime. Life on a continuum. And so it was.

With pre-natal activity and post-natal responses, we gained, and brought forward, wounds. Those wounds unhealed from previous lifetimes appeared in new symptoms and configurations. We might have experienced colic, pain, feeling of rejection, aloneness, insecurity, instability, or health and ability to thrive challenges. The consequences of these early experiences, themselves, a result of prior lifetimes, created chaos for many, and may have contributed to our sense of being welcome in the world we had just entered.

Lessons of life begin early. Acceptance or rejection; Love or absence of love; Pain or comfort; Ease or dis-ease; Life as a flow or life with challenges and interruptions. All of this was recorded in consciousness. All of this, and subsequent lessons, were healed, or recorded within the body-mind-spirit.

Upon reaching adulthood, and sometimes before, these recordings in our mind-body-spirit may become troublesome, and signal a need for healing. All healing of the body follows healing of the spirit. All healing of the mind accelerates this healing. Thus, healing of the mind-body-spirit is required for these recordings of pain, abuse, or uncaring, to be erased.

Healing is a life-long journey, and not a single destination. Healing occurs in waves when one is ready. As old emotions emerge, they can be healed. As the healing occurs and the person regains equilibrium, the next wave is prepared. Therefore, healing of the mind-body-spirit is lifelong. New wounds that remain unhealed become apparent in the next generation. That is why you may see generations of abuse within a family. It continues until one says, "Enough!" And the healing begins.

When lives are short, it is tragic for families and loved ones. Humans cannot see the bigger Plan, and understand that what was needed was accomplished within this short time-frame.

All humans experience physical and emotional pain. It is the healing of these prior, and present, injuries that is the lesson of that lifetime. It may come in the form of loss, injury, illness, and many variations of these, but healing these challenges through Love energy is the lesson. One cannot heal addiction, for example, by simply removing the addict from the substance. All of the emotional injury and confusion that preceded the addiction still exist. Therefore, true healing of addiction requires acceptance of Love energy to allow all of the wounds—mental, emotional, and physical—to heal. It is lack of Love that leads to addiction, and it is acceptance of Love that leads back to health.

Life is not an Empty Slate

We enter into this lifetime carrying unhealed wounds from previous lifetimes. Each lifetime is an opportunity to heal wounds from the past and the present. Indeed, wounds in the present are in reality re-woundings in need of healing.

Life is a series of events. Each lifetime contains joy and sorrow, pain and relief, lies and truths. It is the person who must learn what is right and true, and what is only masked as truth.

A baby learns, or is unable to learn, trust. Trust is stability. It sets up expectations for repetition. If one experiences another as trustworthy, it creates the expectation that the other may be trusted again. In the event that trust is broken, the sense of having been betrayed can be devastating.

When one looks in the mirror, one sees oneself. After many repetitions, one expects to see oneself as he or she has previously appeared. Accidents and illness can change one's appearance and the way that one sees oneself. That betrayal may send one seeking for new or improved identity. The soul craves reliability and must adjust for change. Thus, illness requires healing, not only of the body, but also the mind and emotions.

The location of each lifetime is carefully prepared and selected for the lessons of that lifetime. A lifetime of abundance may be followed by a lifetime of simplicity or even scarcity. This teaches the value of the soul as being complete without the trappings of one's culture.

Therefore, you may see people who seem to have acquired little in the physical world, yet who have character and personality full of love, caring and joy.

You may see others who have much in the way of comfort and society's definition of success, yet are depressed and angry. They are often empty, and lacking the connection to Love that brings true fulfillment. Unless they are able to be vulnerable and surrender their lives to Love, they will continue their own self-destruction. This can be most upsetting to family and friends who know how to relieve their pain, but cannot penetrate the walls built to retain their misery. Many will only heal in a future lifetime.

Love heals, and is available to all who seek it and open themselves to acceptance. Denial of Love continues one on an eventual desperate track. It is each person's right to choose. Free will means that one may accept or reject Love. Lack of Love leads to the deterioration of the mind-body, and recovery may not occur in the present lifetime.

When one continues to deny Love energy, their deterioration affects the family and friend network meant to support each person. It creates pain for each person to heal. Therefore, that person becomes toxic to all who surround them. Those who are pained must then heal their wounds, sometimes in spite of the lack of healing in the one who refuses Love. Therefore, addictions and destructive behaviors affect the family and friend system, creating pain and suffering that often require a lifetime of Love and healing.

Humans are interconnected. Once joined in relationship, the actions of one affect all others. Therefore, destruction of oneself or others creates a climate of distrust and pain that requires time and Love energy to heal.

Healing of the Body Requires Healing of the Mind.

Your Healers work to diffuse painful memories in the emotional and mental bodies. Energy accrues in the body that causes one to feel unwell. Often the symptoms are mild or sporadic at first, but if not attended to, become more severe. Accumulation of negative energies in the body over time creates an unwell condition leading to disease. Disease is the unwellness of the mind-emotional bodies made manifest.

Dis-ease of the mental-emotional body has many manifestations. It can occur in a part of the body often related to the unease. Anxiety is caused by living in a potential future that is painful, or dangerous. It is not living in the present moment. Dis-ease of the joint is caused by painful memories associated with previous accidents, illness, or abuse. In general, the negative energy forms in the location associated with the memory. This is not always the case, but is a clue to the Healer when attempting to dissipate negative energy, thereby preventing illness.

When you entered the world, you came with a history from previous incarnations. In each incarnation, if the opportunity to heal is not seized and accomplished, the negative patterns follow into succeeding incarnations. Thus, the Invitation to Love is given in each incarnation, offering the opportunity for healing to occur.

In the beginning there was energy. It materialized into the universe as you understand it. Humans are but a micro-universe within the larger universe. All return to the Energy from which they came.

Universal Energy for Healing

The employment of Universal Energy for healing is in need of clarification. Your people may have good intentions for the well-being of another, yet they have not mastered this gift.

Universal energy is available to all, but few understand how to access it. People often ask: Is Energy good or evil? For what purpose can it be used? Is it possible to hurt another through the use of Universal Energy? How does it heal?

We are here to tell you that you are playing with Energy like a child with a toy. You know some of its power, but not how to use it safely and effectively. We will explain.

Universal Energy is the author and designer of the life of the Universe. This Universe is energy. You are energy. All that you perceive is energy. Life-energy is the movement of energy in all human life. That changes at the moment you call death. In actuality, death is the movement of life-energy from one universe into another.

Intention provides the direction and focus of energy. If it is being intentionally directed toward healing, the process will be accelerated, but not changed. In other words, if healing is to be within the body, the body will experience more rapid change. If healing is to be beyond the body, that process will also be expedited. In the latter, the person who is ill will begin having experiences in preparation for this transition. Therefore, when you pray, do so in the absence of preference as you cannot control the outcome.

As humans advance in their understanding of healing with Universal Energy, they will be humbled by the recognition that life has endings and beginnings as part of the greater Plan.

Consider employing Universal Energy in other areas. It can remove internal blockages to one's success, provide guidance, and energize depleted physical condition. It can move one to be open to other opportunities. It can advise one whether to go forward, maintain, or retreat as a decision. It promotes personal effectiveness by assisting one to know whom to trust and whom to avoid.

Universal Energy is employed when we choose to see a "glass half full." It propels one in a positive direction, while focusing on the negative gives negative direction a boost.

Humans did not, do not, create energy. They cannot control Energy, however they can direct and focus it.

Moriah had such an experience. When she saw pairs of eyes during a meditative state of consciousness, she immediately recognized them as the "Grays", and commanded them to "Go Away!" They responded immediately and disappeared from view.

During energy Healing sessions with Moriah, clients reported out of body feelings and deep relaxation. Energy can be a tool to help others teleport to other levels of consciousness.

However, Universal Energy can be used to harm when used with negative intention. Moriah experienced energy abuse at the hands of a healer when in that moment of misunderstanding, the heart of the healer was filled with anger.

When employing or sending Universal Energy, recognize Its ability to cause disruption and change. Prayers for peace may be answered with a sword of truth before there can be peace. Evil thoughts manifest as horrors in individual lives and in all humanity. Thoughts have intention. Wishing evil on another contributes to the grief and sadness in your world. Change your thoughts, and behaviors, to those that are beneficial to self and others to help promote peace.

Unity promotes Universal Healing. Unity is the focused intentions of many toward the raising of humanity's vibration toward peace.

Human will is full of intentionality. Speak only of love and unity to evoke the highest vibration of Universal Energy.

What is Healing?

Healing is the final resolution with Love. It is the moment when all pain and suffering are released. It is a glorious moment when one awakens to newness all around. There is a familiarity of recognition of loved ones who previously passed. It is a time of unity and joy as one remembers one's Source and previous lifetimes.

After rest and renewal, new options are given as one's progress toward Love is assessed. One does not fail; one assesses lessons learned. Scenarios are provided for one's next adventure. One has many choices, and may choose to rest, or to move forward with new challenges. One chooses who will accompany one on the next journey. Other relationships are temporarily released until one may join again with "family" from previous lifetimes.

Those relationships that one will bring into one's next lifetime are chosen. Each will have a role. Lessons will be learned within this family unit that will move one farther on one's spiritual journey. The Invitation to Love will again be given. One will again choose whether to follow Love, or to attempt to manage one's life alone. Yet, in reality, one is never alone.

This cycle of lives continues for each Being until one has become one with One. It is a beautiful Plan as all will eventually join.

Do not allow fears of loss and death to overwhelm you. Love encompasses all life. All life is part of Universal Love. All will eventually join.

V. Moriah's Healing Journey

"Make me a channel of Your Love and Peace through eternity ......"

Healing begins with surrender ......

Healing Surrender

I surrender

  my will to Your Will
  my wants to Your Desire
  my understanding to Your Understanding
  my self to my Self
  my plans to the greater Plan
  my life to Your Service
  my heart to Your Love
  my fear to Your Peace.

When the evening of my life is near
  I pray I will have completed my Purpose
    Your Purpose for my life.

Thank you for

  Life, Love, Family, Friends, Understanding, Purpose

  A Life to Live for You

  A Purpose to give for You.

Love is all
Love is the greater Plan
Love is evolution
Love is

Remembering my first Experience
Consoling me at a time of loss
Letting me feel Your Energy
Letting me know You were there

So many times I've felt You
    in the Energy that envelops me
    in the Voice that bids me there
    in the sights of nature
    and the warmth of Love

So many times
Yet, in my humanity, I still doubt, I still fear, I still tremble
But when I feel alone, You are there.
Even more.
Evermore

—Moriah

Healing Message of Love

The healing began, and I understood my pain.

Now I release my pain, and understand.

Forgiveness is the key to health and healing.

Anger at oneself is the source of all pain.

Release the anger, and healing begins.

Healing is a journey, not a destination.

Pain returns only to be released again.

When it returns, it is a warning

That there is still unfinished healing to do.

Face the challenge with trust and understanding

That you can face the anger once again.

Forgive the offender; forgive yourself.

It is the message of Love.

—Moriah

Healing Evolution

Trying to live in the now
    And not allow anxiety to overwhelm me.

Hoping for good news
    And prepared to go forward anyway.

Without a crystal ball
    We live hoping for the best.

If we attract what we emanate
    I am multiply blessed.

Whenever I think everything is cleared
    I get new lessons.

And so, I still evolve.

—Moriah

Healing My Soul

My heart is filled with gratitude as I reach inside for hidden resources laying in wait.

What I took for granted most of life is now my great challenge.

To walk again will mean inclusion in life's activities--gatherings, travel, speaking out, representing.

It's been a life lesson to learn that it's difficult to live life from the sidelines.

So many live lives of isolation: Those who

> are disabled of all ages
> have chronic pain and fatigue
> are mentally ill
> are living with addictions
> are not accepted by society
> have contagious or incurable diseases

So many watch and yearn, remembering when it was otherwise
    And wishing for more.

Now I will understand.
Whether I walk again, or not
    I will know
Because I'm one with them.

—Moriah

Heal Me

Heal me, I asked
    because I had not asked for myself.

Heal me, the Angels heard.
    Were They surprised?

Heal me, I prayed
    When I stopped thinking only of others.

Heal me, I cried
    Because I had waited so long.

Heal me, I moaned
    When life felt like "too much!"

Heal me, I sought
    When I accepted my vulnerability.

Heal me? I asked
    When I began to feel worthy.

Heal me, too, I prayed
    after asking for others.

Heal me, it echoed
    Across the universe so vast.

Heal me, it vibrated
    Jangling nerves unused to prayer.

Heal me? I asked
    Could it also be for me?

Heal me, I sighed
    When I finally understood.

Heal me, she exclaimed
    It pealed from rafters!

Heal me, she cried
    When pain of not changing became too great.

Heal me, she whispered
    Magnified by all the Angels round.

Heal me, she thought
    It's all that is left.

Heal me..........
    For I need Love.

Heal me.........
    If someone still cares.

Heal me.........
    If not too late.

Heal me..........
    And help me grow.

Heal me!
    She commanded to anyone who'd listen.

Heal me!
    She shouted to All out of sight.

Heal me! ....
    For I now I must do my Purpose.

Heal me! ....
    Until my last breath here is given.

Heal me.........
    For I am now completely Yours.

—Moriah

I Believe in Love

I believe
    in the inherent goodness of every person
    every person has a choice
    each person chooses to follow Love or fear
    each person receives increased energy to expand
        upon that choice

I believe
    that as Love energy fills one, choices become clear
    Love energy is magnified
    Love clears a path and casts all that is not in
        alignment
    as Love clears, old negativity surfaces

I believe
    that negativity is exposed for the purpose of healing
    that dark energy must come into the Light
    that as dark energy is exposed, physical
        manifestations present for healing
    that healing purifies one for service

I believe
    that Love requires continuous healing
    that Love clears out darkness to make room for
        Light
    that Light Beings lighten the world's darkness
    that Light exposes darkness where it hides

I believe
> that Light Beings serve Love
> that Love energy exposes darkness
> that dark energy can and will be healed
> that our planet is coming back into the Light

—Moriah

At Peace

I am at Peace.
Life is not easy.
Friends and family are leaving
And they won't be coming back.

I am at Peace
'Though the world is rumbling
Expressing distaste
At bullies and fear.

I am at Peace
'Though I see so much pain
'Though I feel temporary
Even as I know I am not.

I am at Peace
'Though the diagnoses multiply
'Though resources dwindle
I am at Peace.

I accepted the Invitation to Love
And now only Love is enough.

Even pain is temporary.

—Moriah

Commitment

The Purification came
> and I am healed

Today I thank God
> Who has healed me

Today I realize
> that Love heals

Today I understand
> what I am to do

Today I once again
> Commit to my Purpose and Calling in the world

—Moriah

Gratitude for Being

I am thankful for my brain, the control center for my body. It allows me to think beautiful thoughts, enjoy scenic vistas, feel the wind in my hair and the sun on my skin.

I am thankful for my bosom. It has hugged and nursed my children, cushioned those in pain, and carried little ones from danger.

I am thankful for my arms. They add power to my piano music through the depths of my muscles. They have carried babies, puppies, and all of life's burdens. They have held the sick and reached out to the dying. They extend from my body to connect with others.

I am thankful for my lips. They have reassured children and elderly, taught in classrooms and auditoriums, carried messages of hope, and messages of peace.

I am thankful for my nose. It has carried my breath, bringing life to all my organs. It has warned of danger and sought food as energy. It precedes and guides, though is seldom recognized. I love my nose.

I am thankful for my hair. It provides protection from both heat and cold. It cradles me, yet expresses me. It can be carefree or uptight. It reflects my moods and presents a first impression.

I am thankful for my stomach. It receives food and converts it to energy that I may go, do, serve, enjoy. It makes life possible. I love my stomach.

I am thankful for my back. It has carried me through the years and miles of life. It has stood straight when attacked, bristled when appalled, and suffered under weights too painful to bear. It supports me without thought, takes abuse from daily chores, and then rests and recovers to carry me through another day.

I am thankful for my legs. They carry me where I desire, and rest to serve me another day. When tired and arthritic from years of use, they submit to treatments to help them continue. Always wanting to meet my needs, they keep moving even when they long to rest. I love my legs.

I am thankful for my fingers. They have endured years of exercises to be able to play beautiful music, yet caress a child or the ill or wounded. They send vital information to my brain, and protect me and others by doing so. They can recognize a fever or a fire, recoil from freezing, and brush aside cares. I love my fingers.

I am thankful for my feet and toes. They balance and carry me. They tolerate the pounding of weight for years, and are resilient for yet more. They take me to places only dreamed of by many. They feel the sand and water that make my heart thrill.

I am thankful for my heart. It beats thanklessly, taken for granted at every breath. It circulates my life blood, and carries that life to my whole body. Thank you, my heart. I love you most of all.

I am thankful for my Mind for it is far greater than my brain. It is my soul connection to the Divine, and life unending. It has carried me through many lifetimes in many places. It is all I truly am, my body simply a temporary manifestation. It contains all memories, and expands for more. It is I, yet greater than I. It is, and connects to the Divine of which I, as each of us, am a part. It is the beginning without end. It is consciousness. It is soul. It is higher self. It is who I truly am. It is who We each truly are.

And so, We continue, together.

--Moriah

VI. *Benediction*

As you leave this place of serenity and solitude,
As you raise your hearts to Love,
   take with you the solemn commitment to devote yourselves-
         your lives, your efforts,
         your complete existence--to Love.

Love heals.
Love unites.
Love lifts.
Love guides.
Love joins all, who would accept, to everlasting love.

Think not that you are enjoined for your own purpose.
You are enjoined to bring forth Love into the world.
The world cries out for Love.
It is you, the spiritual sojourner, who must answer the call, and serve.

Let Love be your guide in all decisions.
Let Love light your way.
Let Love be all you seek,
         all you experience,
         all you express.
Now, and always.

   The Presence of the Teachers of Love is with us.

                                                     –Moriah

My Healing Journey

www.ingramcontent.com/pod-product-compliance
Lightning Source LLC
Chambersburg PA
CBHW060203050426
42446CB00013B/2973